Puffin Books

Who's Who at the Zoo

Chimpanzee
up a tree
looks like you
not like me.

Full of sharp-eyed observations of all the
wild and wonderful creatures at the zoo,
this delightful collection of comical verse
combines wit and word-play with a host
of vibrant illustrations.

Poetry by the same author

Gnome Sweet Gnome
That's Us

Poems by
Celeste Walters

Illustrated by
Patricia Mullins

Puffin Books

Puffin Books
Penguin Books Australia Ltd
487 Maroondah Highway, PO Box 257
Ringwood, Victoria 3134, Australia
Penguin Books Ltd
Harmondsworth, Middlesex, England
Viking Penguin, A Division of Penguin Books USA Inc.
375 Hudson Street, New York, New York 10014, USA
Penguin Books Canada Limited
10 Alcorn Avenue, Toronto, Ontario, Canada M4V 3B2
Penguin Books (N.Z.) Ltd
182–190 Wairau Road, Auckland 10, New Zealand

First published by Penguin Books Australia Ltd, 1996
10 9 8 7 6 5 4 3 2 1
Copyright © Celeste Walters, 1996
Illustrations Copyright © Patricia Mullins, 1996

All rights reserved. Without limiting the rights under copyright reserved above, no part of this publication may be reproduced, stored in or introduced into a retrieval system, or transmitted, in any form or by any means (electronic, mechanical, photocopying, recording or otherwise), without the prior written permission of both the copyright owner and the above publisher of this book.

Typeset in 13/16pt Bembo
Made and printed in Australia by Australian Print Group

National Library of Australia
Cataloguing-in-Publication data:

Walters, Celeste.
 Who's who at the zoo.

ISBN 0 14 038318 2.

1. Zoo animals – Juvenile poetry. 2. Children's poetry, Australian. I. Mullins, Patricia, 1952- . II. Title

For Graham,

and also

*Wee Willie Bones,
who thought only cats were killed by curiosity*

— C.W. —

For my sister, Jennie

— P.M. —

Foreword

Some time ago, on a cold and wintry day, I took the train to the zoo. I wandered the fern-edged paths, watching creatures at rest, at play, eating, interacting, being bossy, argumentative, loving, playful. I noticed that some animals behaved the way I have seen some people behave, so in my notebook, that's how I wrote of them. And as some breathed quietly in sleep, I imagined what they might be thinking. Dreaming. I went on to have fun playing with names and words and sometimes, to be even more waggish, I took liberties with spelling. I asked questions also – like what would happen if you bathed a hippopotamus or were bitten by a bittern?

But I was writing always with respect for the true nature of each creature, making sure that the information I used was scientifically correct.

And now, with the notebook full, I would like to pass on the joy of my feelings and encounters to you . . . that you might experience your own.

Celeste Walters

Contents

Spotty Botty 1
Taipan 2
King Cobra 2
Death Adder 3
The Children's Python 3
Bathing Big Smellies 4
Bear Facts 6
The Pademelon 8
Pyjama Llama 9
The Prairie Wolf 9
Dress: Black Tie 10
China Watcher 11
Some Frog! 12
The Spider Monkey 13
Chameleon 13
Out-fox Fox! 14
Grey Squirrel 14
Fruity Agouti 16
Ouch! 16
Gnamed Gnu 17
Bottle Lotl 18
Sour Puss 19
The Painted Lady 19

Platypus	19
Mammoth Mammoth	20
Chimpanzee	23
OlympiFred	24
Ah-choo!	25
ShrewIcide	26
The Crocodile	26
The Barn Owl	27
Fearty Fiend	28
The Prairie Dog	29
Dear Deer	29
Kooky Burra	30
Rhino O'Mine-o	31
Whoops!	32
Go Anna!	33
The Potoroo	33
How Much Can a Grizzly Bear?	34
Fur Consideration	34
Alligator	35
Beware the Cheetah	36
Pale Yellow Eye	37
The Tapir	39
The Jackal	40
The Royal Spoonbill	41
Numbat	42

Wombat	43
Armadillo Pillow	43
Cute Coot	44
Kowari	45
He's the Hero	46
Opossum	48
Koala	49
Lolly Poss	49
Kangaroo	49
Saucy Songster	50
Carrot Parrot	51
The Camel	53
Don't Badger a Badger	54
The Condor	54
Beak Freak	55
Snifter Beastie	56
The Komodo Dragon	56
Cruellest Rulest	57
Mr Giraffe	59
Hyena	60
Bon Appétit	60
Unleaded Flyer	61
The Quail	61
Preen Clean	61

Achiever Beaver 62
The Dingo 62
Aspiration 62
Yakko! 63
Whoosh! 64
The Ostbridge 65
Lynx Jinx 66
Who am I? 67
Drag Jag 68
The Peccary 69
Pet Toilette 70
The Bettong 71
Mousework 71
Main Part 72
Matters Editorial 74
Purpose Porpoise 76
The Wolf 77
Eggs a-Poppin' 77

Spotty Botty

The large-toothed baboon
is inclined
to advertise his rude behind
still I don't mind if he don't mind
but I can't speak for all mankind.

Taipan

Deadly taipan
in a frypan
looks ornamental
tastes oriental.

King Cobra

When king cobra lifts its hood
you know that it's up to no good
so be advised before you carkit
buy a mongoose at the market.

Death Adder

Death adder
nothing badder
though a curse
is sometimes worse.

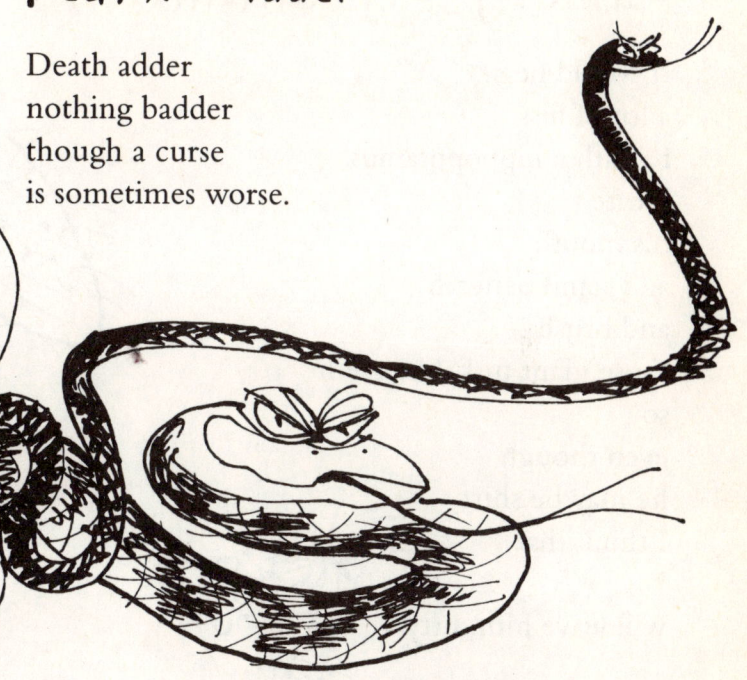

The Children's Python

The children's python
likes to eat
green frogs and birds and lizard meat
but on his birthday
'stead of toys
his friends give him some girls and boys.

Bathing Big Smellies

It would be
a lot of fuss
to bath a hippopotamus
locate
his mouth
and stand beneath
and brush
those giant tusk-like teeth
so
even though
he may be shirty
I think that
I
will leave him dirty.

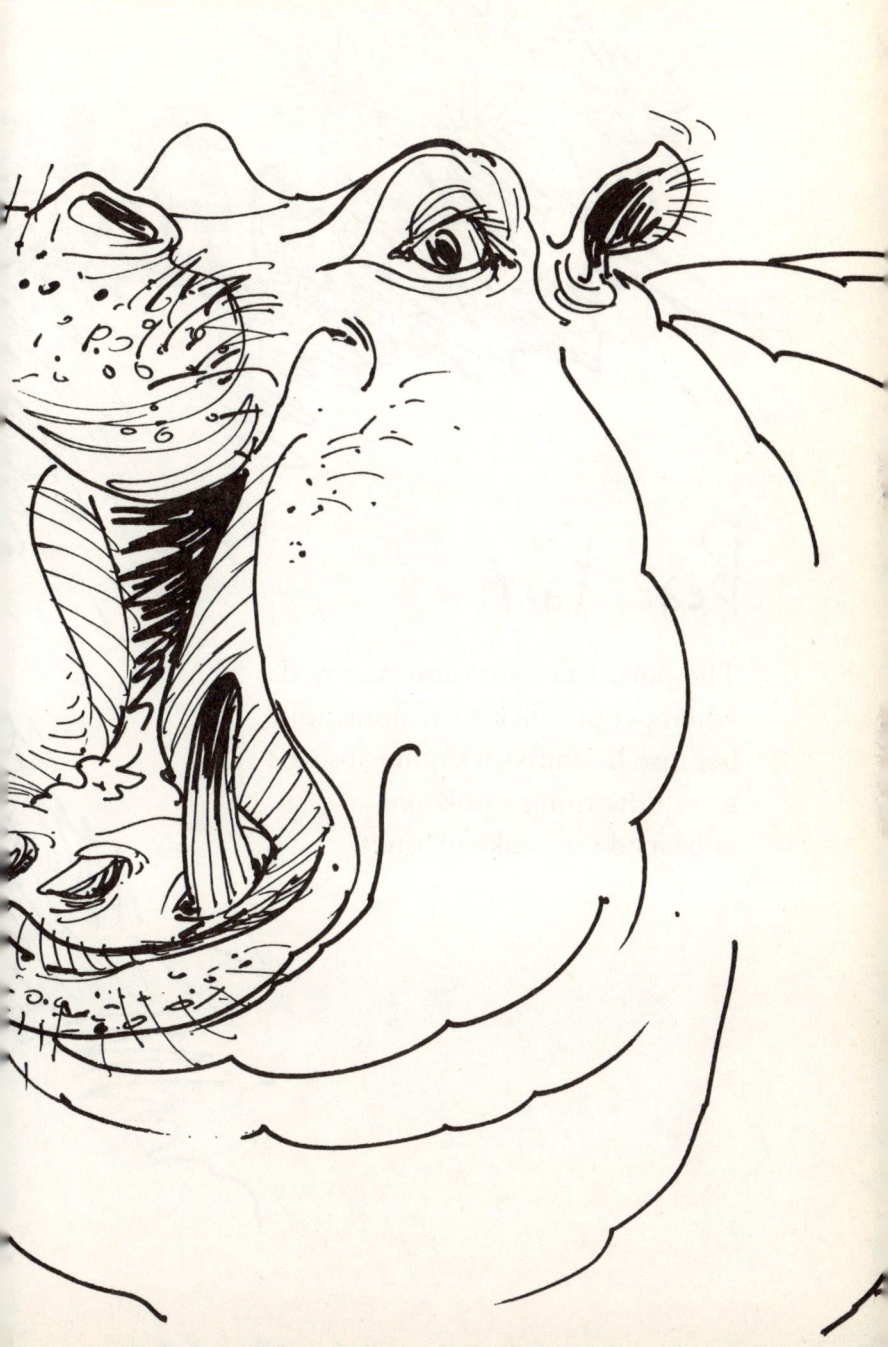

Bear Facts

The polar bear gets quite annoyed
when people click their humanoid
because he thinks it's quite absoyed
to call the thing a polaroid
as bears do not take pictures.

The Pademelon

The pademelon
has a dream
of being served up
with ice-cream.

Pyjama Llama

It's very awkward for a llama
to dress in a warm pyjama
or pyjamas I suppose
of flannel patterned with a rose
for when he buys them in a store
he finds two legs and nothing more
and so he either, with a scoff,
deftly screws his hind legs off
or otherwise with caution weaves
his two front legs inside the sleeves
and then he's ready for the night
and with his nose turns out the light.

The Prairie Wolf

The prairie wolf with smiling eyes
is known as the coyote
and likely when you say gidday
to grab you by the throatee.

Dress: Black Tie

If you are asked to dinner
by a penguin it is normal
to get your best regalia out
because the evening's formal

you can guarantee all comers
will flip in when daylight pales
dressed in freshly laundered waistcoats
shining footwear and black tails.

China Watcher

The black-eyed panda sees around 'er black-eyed masses in sun-glasses.

Some Frog!

The trilling frog
is trilling
'cos the female thinks it's thrilling.

The Spider Monkey

The slender spider monkey
has a tail that is prehensile
which for swinging through the trees
is a most valuable utensil.

Chameleon

Chameleon can change his hue
a hundred times a day
present a new persona
to whoever comes his way
by this means he can plot and plan
with jolly repetition
I think that the chameleon
should be a politician.

Out-fox Fox!

The fox instead of running
should employ its native cunning
and with the sound of horn and hound
like the ferret go to ground.

Grey Squirrel

Grey squirrel
hibernates
so do
all its mates
the habit is
quite natural
but
I think the squirrel
is a nut.

Fruity Agouti

Don't finance
an agouti
for its booty
is but fruity.

Ouch!

If you feed
the little bittern
you might get
a little bittern.

Gnamed Gnu

A wildebeest is a gnu
did you gno?
'cos I gnu
a wildebeest is a gnu
but the gnu
does he gno
what I gno
and you gno?
does the wildebeest gno
like we gno
he's a gnu?

Bottle Lotl

If you throttle
axolotl
stuff it gently
in a bottle
charge a dollar for a gander
(for it's a nice salamander)
people will say
thanksalotl
he's as smart as
Aristotle.

Sour Puss

The native cat that's called a quoll
in spite of feline protocol
is fierce, aggressive, full of vice
and really isn't very nice.

The Painted Lady

Light on a petal, flit gaily around
flutterby, butterfly, gossamer gown'd.

Platypus

Pusses are catty
and platys are pussy
if that isn't natty
then you are just fussy.

Mammoth Mammoth

Archaistic
neolithic
antediluvian
beast
were you conceived
in some strange dream
of ears and wings
and trees of figs
and galleons at sea?
was that the case
you antiquarian
proboscidean
elephant?
will you survive then
at man's hand
beneath a greenie's banner?
or will you finish up as keys
upon a grand pianer?

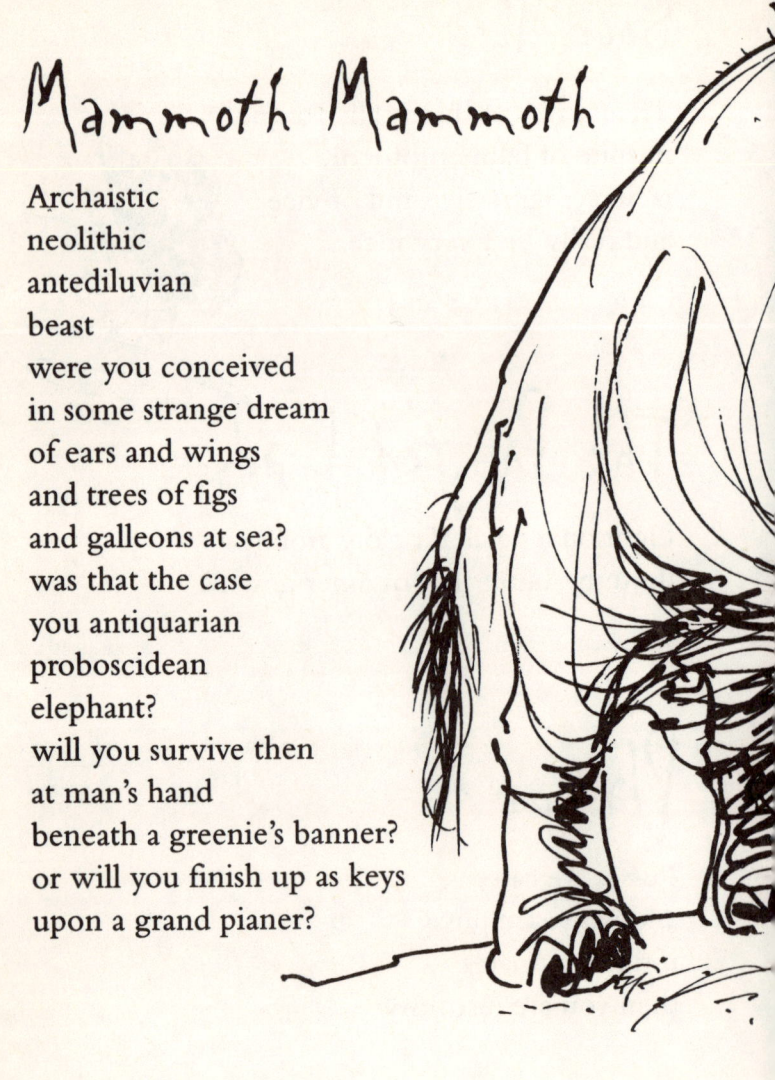

Chimpanzee

Chimpanzee
up a tree
looks like you
not like me.

OlympiFred

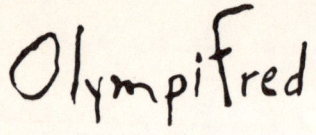

This pinniped
whose name is Fred
backstrokes
trackstrokes
trains for gold
this pinniped
whose name is Fred
has fish each meal
'cos he's a seal.

Ah-choo!

Be careful – if you catch a cuckoo you might get a common koel.

ShrewICIDE

This pair of tree shrew
if they're in a bad mood
will not hesitate
to kill off their whole brood.

The Crocodile

The crocodile
sunbakes awhile
with sweetly smiling jaws
it once was hunted for its skin
and now it hunts for yours.

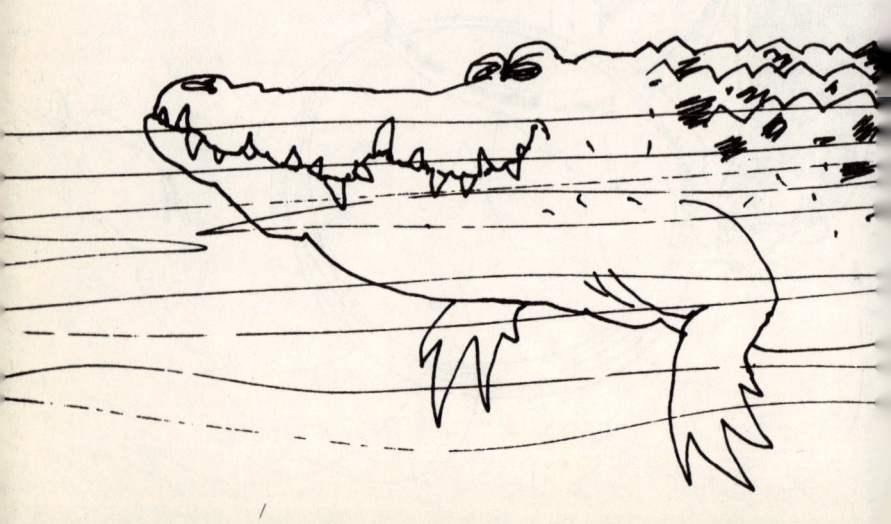

The Barn Owl

The wise barn owl
without a grunt
can turn its head
from back to front
this may be wise
although the knack's
confusing when
its front's its back.

Fearty Fiend

Tasmanian devil
with fearsome growl
and fearsome eye
and fearsome howl
whenever you shoot him a fearsome look
will run off and hide
'cos he's really a sook.

The Prairie Dog

The prairie dog
is not a dog
although it likes to bark
for it's a large fat rodent
that will bite you in the dark.

Dear Deer

The white-tailed doe says to the buck
in manner apprehensive
'Our babe's not just a little deer
he's really quite expensive.'

Kooky Burra

Laughing kookaburra
you could be a little ho(a)rse
if you go on cac-kl-ing
(and had four legs of course).

Rhino O'Mine-o

The rhino has a hairless skin
and thick hide that folds out and in
and even though he looks gargantuan
and larger than the distant mountuan
he's really shy and inoffensive
with tiny piggy eyes so pensive
and hopes one day that someone prosperous
will make him a pet rhinosperous.

Whoops!

The funny desert porcupine
has knitting needles for a spine
and when it's curled up nice and neat
I'll put it on my grandma's seat.

Go Anna!

Anna Goanna is thought to be manna
by those with entrails that can gobble up scales.

The Potoroo

The potoroo
declares he's not
one-third kanga
two-thirds pot.

How Much Can a Grizzly Bear?

How much can a grizzly bear
when day after day people stare
make remarks at his weight
laugh aloud at his gait
how much can a grizzly bear?

How much can a grizzly bear
when day after day he is there
but if you're at the zoo
and with nothing to do
just tell him a tale
read a poem or two
in a voice that is kind
and then you will find
that much can a grizzly bear.

Fur Consideration

Just think, blue mink, of your potential
if we were not environmential.

Alligator

Alligator
nothing straighter
than the sight of legs and paws
poking out between its jaws.

Beware the Cheetah

Beware the cheetah
if you cheeter
you will not survive
so do not tarry when you meeter
do not doff your hat and greeter
and if you bet at cards and beater
keep in mind that she is fleeter
than all mammals alive
(though I refer with some propriety
only to the land variety)
yes, be warned
do not maltreater
best to play with a mosquiter.

Pale Yellow Eye

Pale yellow eye
in rippling skin
pale yellow eye
of hunter
pale yellow stare
from rippling flesh
impales the victim
sinews coil
spring

death
is yellow
death
is black
death
is the unblinking eye
pale yellow eye
of
tiger.

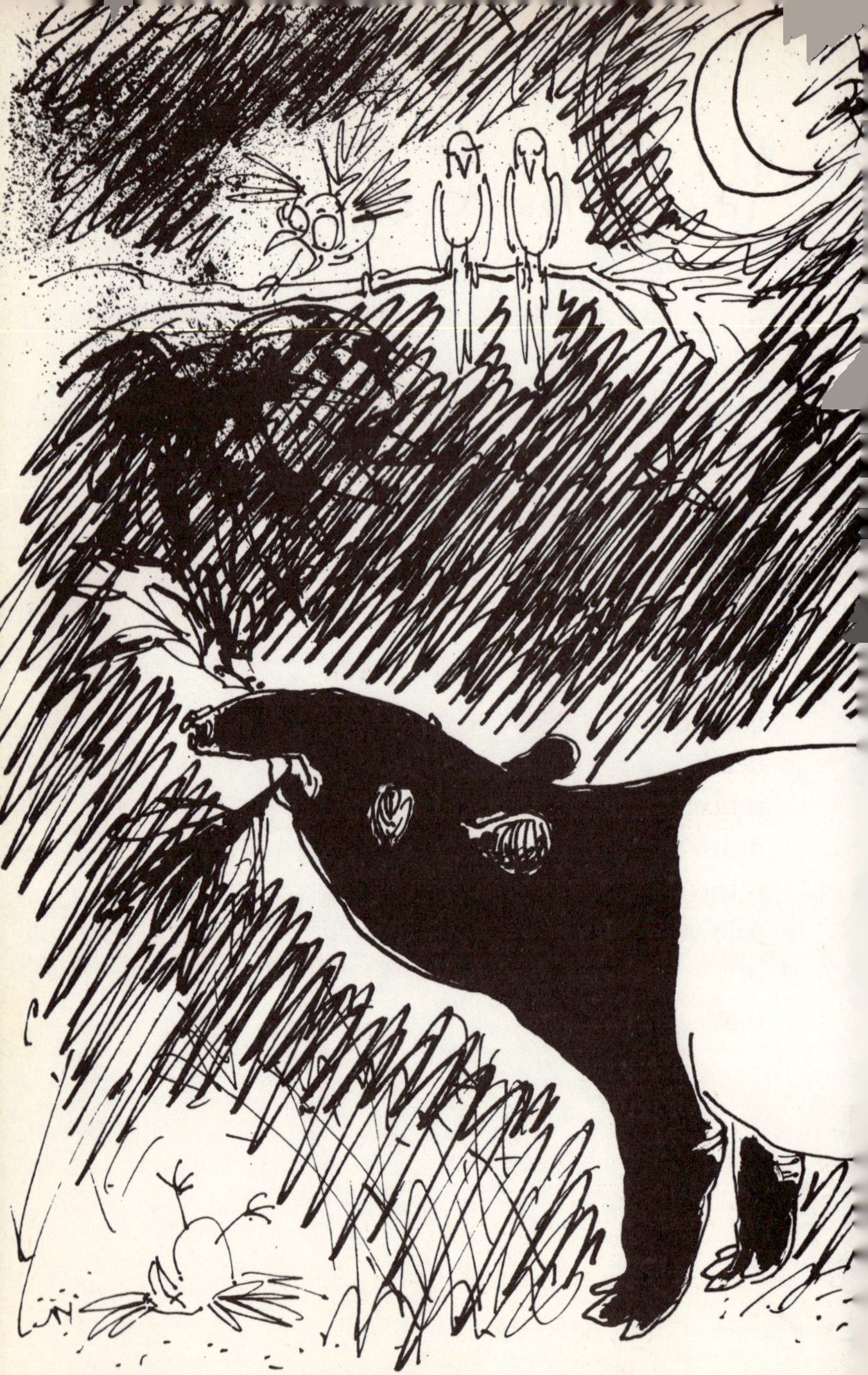

The Tapir

The tapir is the oddest beast
in size just like a donkey
with oval hooves that sprout four toes
and walk that's rather wonky
his tail's a stub
his legs are thick
his ears as smooth as figs
and with his shortened trunk-like snout
he gathers leaves and twigs
and 'cos he's conscious of his looks
he goes about at night
for he's quite right to think you might
take one look
and die of fright.

The Jackal

The jackal is an actor
he is sleek and predatory
and likes to eat his audience
when playing repertory.

The Royal Spoonbill

The royal spoonbill's proud and regal
the waders' version of the eagle
and dreams of flying on a flag
instead of sploshing like a dag.

Numbat

Numbat
larger than a rat
is neither numb
nor blind bat
but master without huff and puffing
of the science of tail-fluffing
not every small marsupial
is as adroit a pupial.

Wombat

Wombat
slow and fat
heavy furry feet a-plodding
massive pig-eyed head a-nodding
dreams upon his wood-log seat
of worlds where wombats are petite.

Armadillo Pillow

The horny-plated armadillo
can be used nightly for a pillow
in case you want to stay awake
or quietly your neck to break
he won't disturb, for he can hold
his breath for minutes, so we're told
and if in seven days or so
you're still alive then simply go
and snuggle close as you can be
until he gives you leprosy
be warned, if you keep armadillo
you had better write your will-o.

Cute Coot

The bandicoot
is very cute
and when it's randy
very bandy.

Kowari

Kowari
quick
marsupial rat
burrows
burrows
shaping furrows
kowari
quick
marsupial rat
hides from the sun
'cos he can't find his hat.

He's the Hero

He's the hero of the great apes
he's the largest strongest primate
and his name is the gorilla
and he's feared in every climate
for his massive head is massive
wire barbs spring from each finger
and I think where a gorilla is
I wouldn't want to linger.

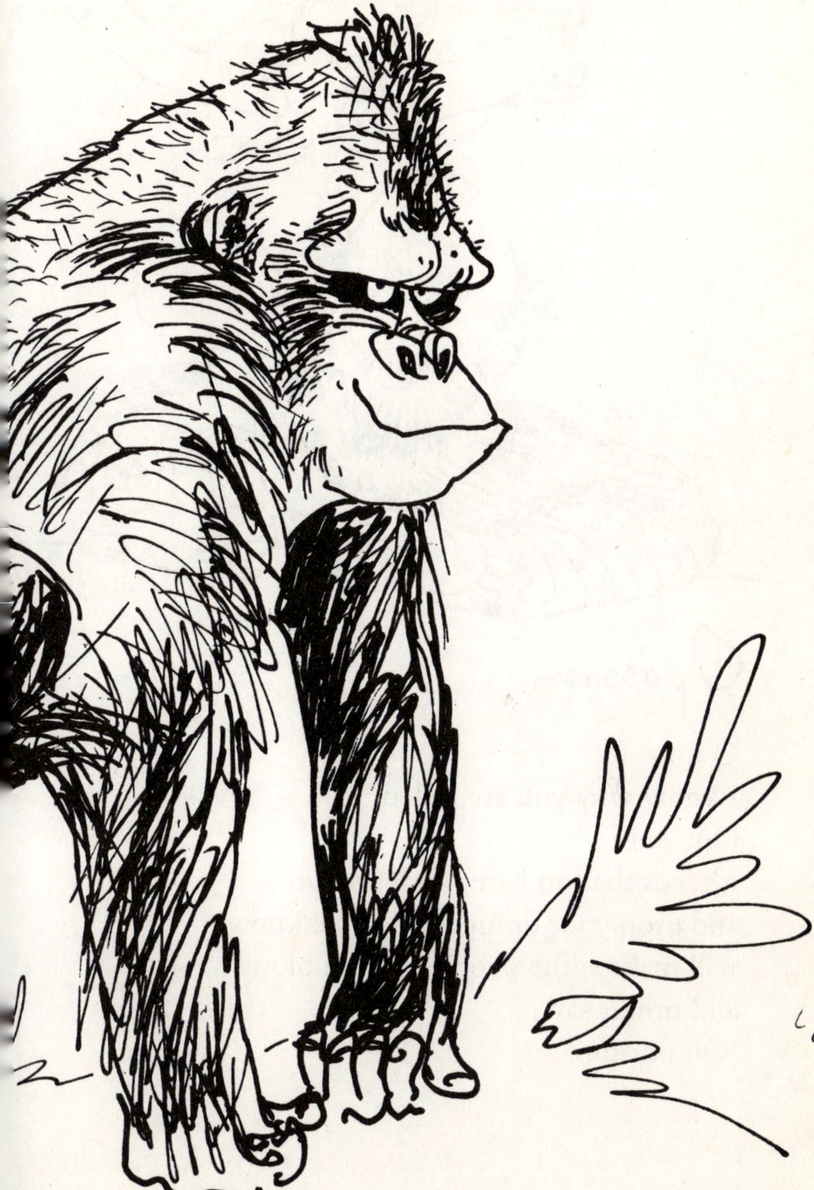

Opossum

O poss
I know why you are called
Opossum
it's 'cos that on bare heads you go
and drop your doings which we know
will make some people say 'Oh blow!'
and others say
'Oh possum!'

Koala

Koala sips his morning tea
that's brewed from tiny tips
selected from the branches
of some tasty eucalypts.

Lolly Poss

Sugar glider
swoop and slider
bat besider
gnat insider.

Kangaroo

Mallee grey
in the way
of squatter's life
and butcher's knife.

Saucy Songster

Eastern rosella
sits of course
on bottles
of tomato sauce.

Carrot Parrot

Do not confuse a carrot
with a double-eyed fig parrot
though both of them are rather red
and both grow green upon their head.

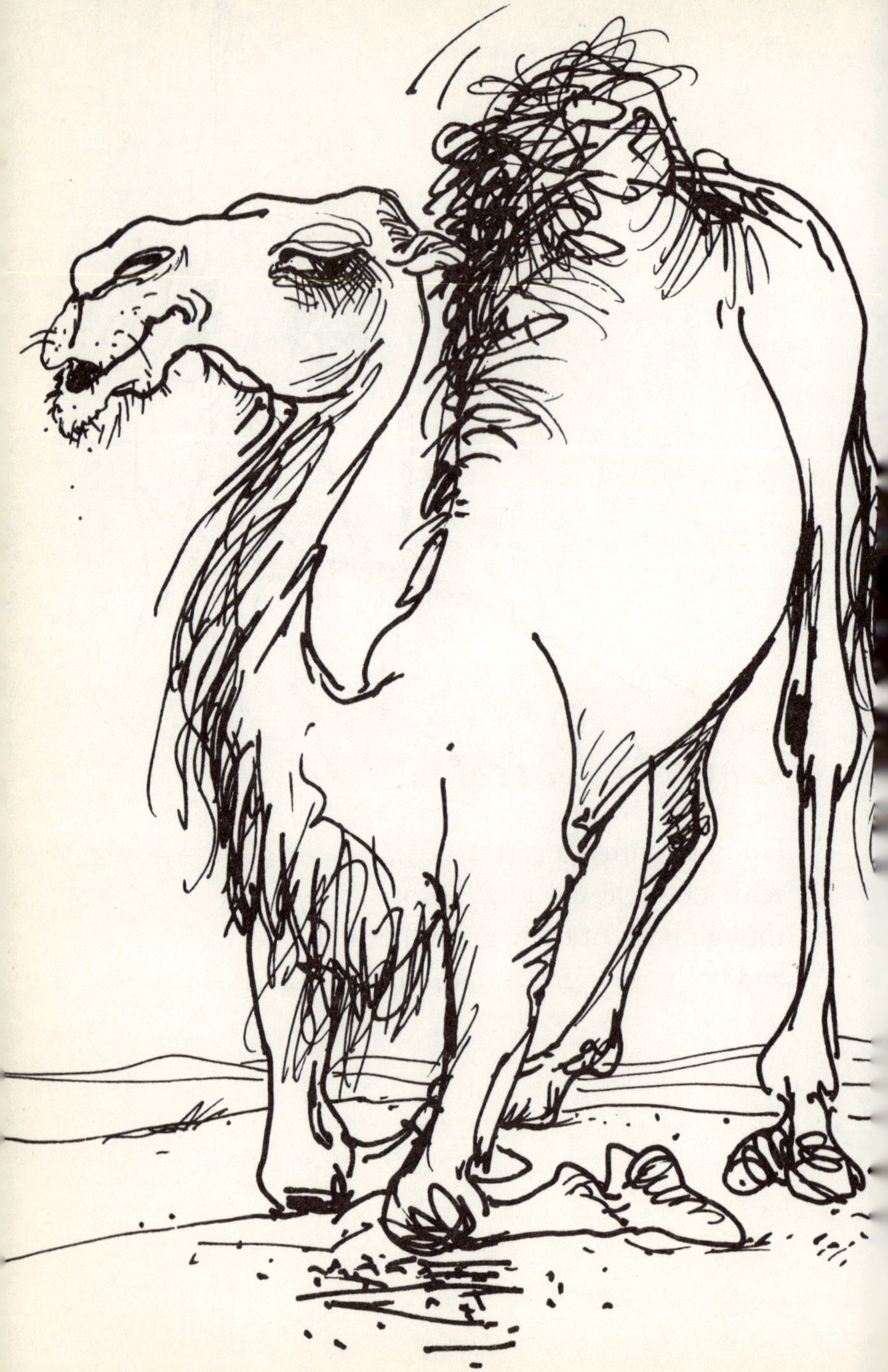

The Camel

The desert heat he can endure
without short sips of aqua pura
run more than fifty ks a day
without a meal upon a tray
describe mirages in the sand
how Aqaba he took by land
and fought (he'll tell with smile that's smarmy)
with El Lawrence in his army
this may be true
this may be not
the camel tends to dream a lot
but that his hump's for storing fat
is simple fact and that is that.

Don't Badger a Badger

Don't badger
a badger
that's no use at all
he'll get in a huff
and just stare at the wall
and if you mistakenly
call him a skunk
he'll get in a terrible
badgery funk
and worse if you're thinking
of being a teasel
and saying that really
he looks like a weasel
he'll go off his black and white
badgery head
and if you're a marmot or squirrel
you're dead.

The Condor

The condor is swooping
the condor eats carrion
so if you feel poorly
you shouldn't be tarrion.

Beak Freak

The pelican will
keep fish in his bill
for it's better basted
before it is tasted.

Snifter Beastie

Eyeless mole
in his hole
finds his clothes
with his nose.

The Komodo Dragon

The Komodo dragon's
the world's largest lizard
with,
sad for the wild pig,
the world's largest gizzard.

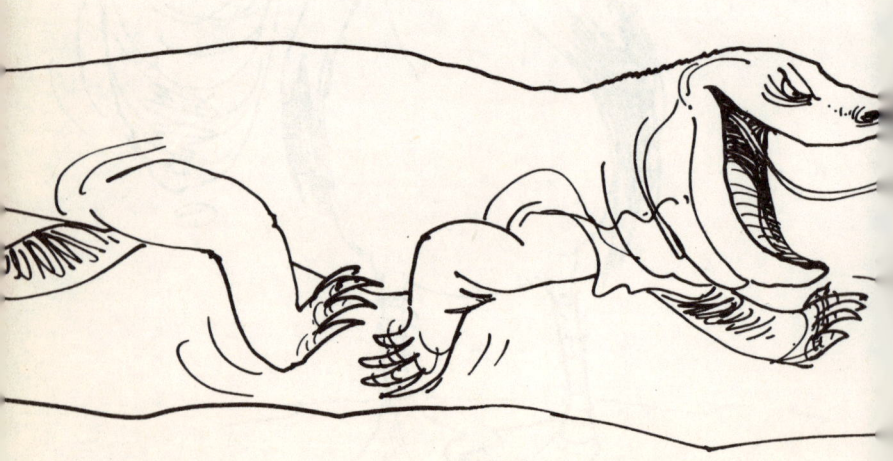

Cruellest Rulest

The mighty lion is the king
the plains are his domain
and over every living beast
he is ordained to reign
he's arrogant he's boastful and
like chauvinists I've known
he gets his wives to catch the meal
while he sits on the throne.

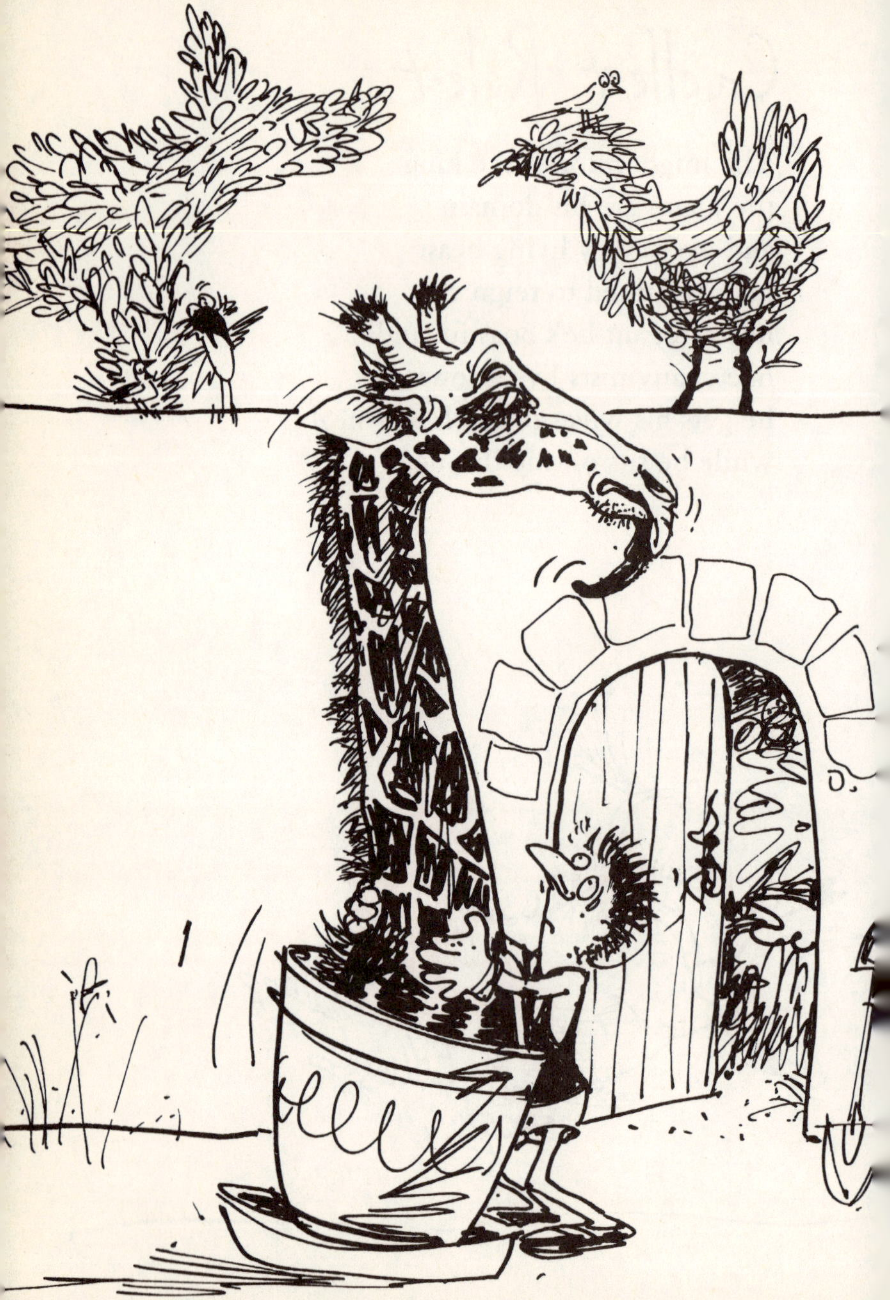

Mr Giraffe

Mr Giraffe
cut in half
is still as tall
as the garden wall.

Hyena

Hyena
grassland vacuum cleaner
sucks up flesh and blood and bones
and leaves a landscape of tombstones.

Bon Appétit

A really nice present
is dinner of pheasant
for all it's most pleasant
except for the pheasant.

Unleaded Flyer

The southern giant petrel
likes fish and meat to eat
it also likes to make your car
go flying down the street.

The Quail

The quail
would quail
if it were able
to see above
the kitchen table.

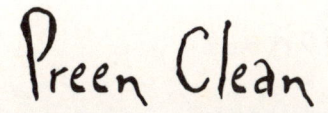

Preen Clean

The heron has a gland called preen
which makes its plumage nice and clean.

Achiever Beaver

If you're working like a beaver
then with front teeth you are gnawing
and in every type of workplace
you will find the job is boring.

The Dingo

The dingo of Australia
has dog-like paraphernalia
but you'd be mad to let him guard
those nice plump chickens in your yard.

ASPiration

I am a happy squirming asp
my forebears writhed with zest
especially the one that nibbled
Cleopatra's breast.

Yakko!

Give a whack
to a yak
if he tries to argue back
make him whinge
pull his fringe
tell him he's a useless pet
and pack him back off to Tibet.

Whoosh!

The flightless, feathered rhea
is so fast
it's hard to see 'er.

The Ostbridge

The ostrich is galumphious
the largest bird alive
and smaller creatures through its legs
their cars and buses drive.

Lynx Jinx

Baby lynx has pointed ears
that pick up everything he hears
and even keener is his sight
those small lynx-eyes pierce blackest night

and on his broad feet he can go
away across the fields of snow
return and cook as is his habit
dinner out of snowshoe rabbit

he looks so cute just like my cat
when dressed up in his tabby clothes
but if I pat him I think that
he'll pounce
and off will come my nose.

Who am I?

What what what
what do you think
would be a tawny frogmouth?
would it be
a cane toad
or a tadpole
or a tawn?
would it be
a paddy
or a melon
or a yawn?
would it be an orange dentist
looking all forlorn?
no no no
now quiet please
the tawny frogmouth's
none of these
though it's absurd
I've overheard
the tawny frogmouth
is
a bird.

Drag Jag

My uncle
keeps a jaguar
locked up in his garage
but I believe
a jaguar
would rather be
at large
or maybe
he'd prefer the zoo
together with
the friends he knew
renounce
the world of racing
for the gentle one
of pacing.

The Peccary

The short-legged collared peccary
has tusks but not much neckary.

Pet Toilette

If I could have a little pet
'twould be a hairy marmoset
a table it would have and chair
I'd tie a ribbon in its hair
its tiny teeth of thirty-two
I'd brush until they looked like new
and then I'd wash and comb its tail
and hang it dry upon a nail.

The Bettong

The bettong
has a problem
he thinks he is a rabbit
because he stamps his hind feet hard
as is his usual habit.

The bettong has a problem
he thinks he is a dog
because he sits and loudly growls
upon a hollow log.

It's hard to be a bettong
who doesn't know who's who
and sees bewilderment on those
who pass him in the zoo.

Mousework

If the hopping mouse
won't do it
then the female says
'Hop to it!'

Main Part

The walrus went for an audition
he posed in the inverse position
and though his children thought him manic
he got the role of the Titanic.

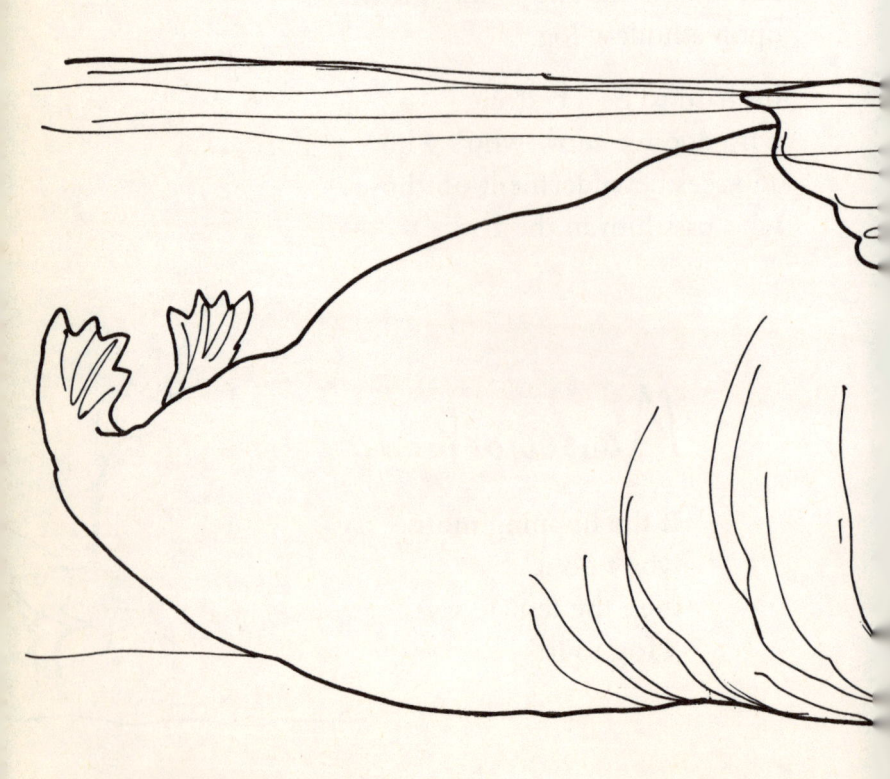

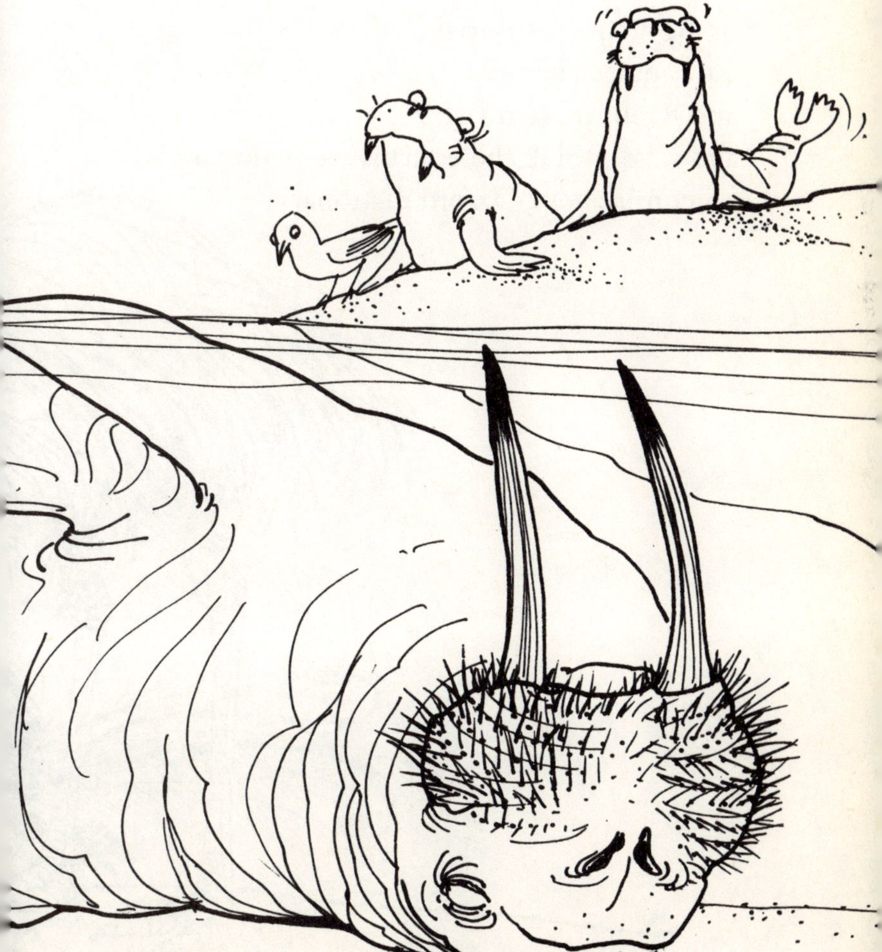

Matters Editorial

The lemur is enchorial
the two-toed sloth, arboreal
whilst vultures are raptorial
orang-utans, scansorial
emus quite cursorial
and lyrebirds, sartorial
and if you think these terms are fictionary
go consult your Oxford dictionary.

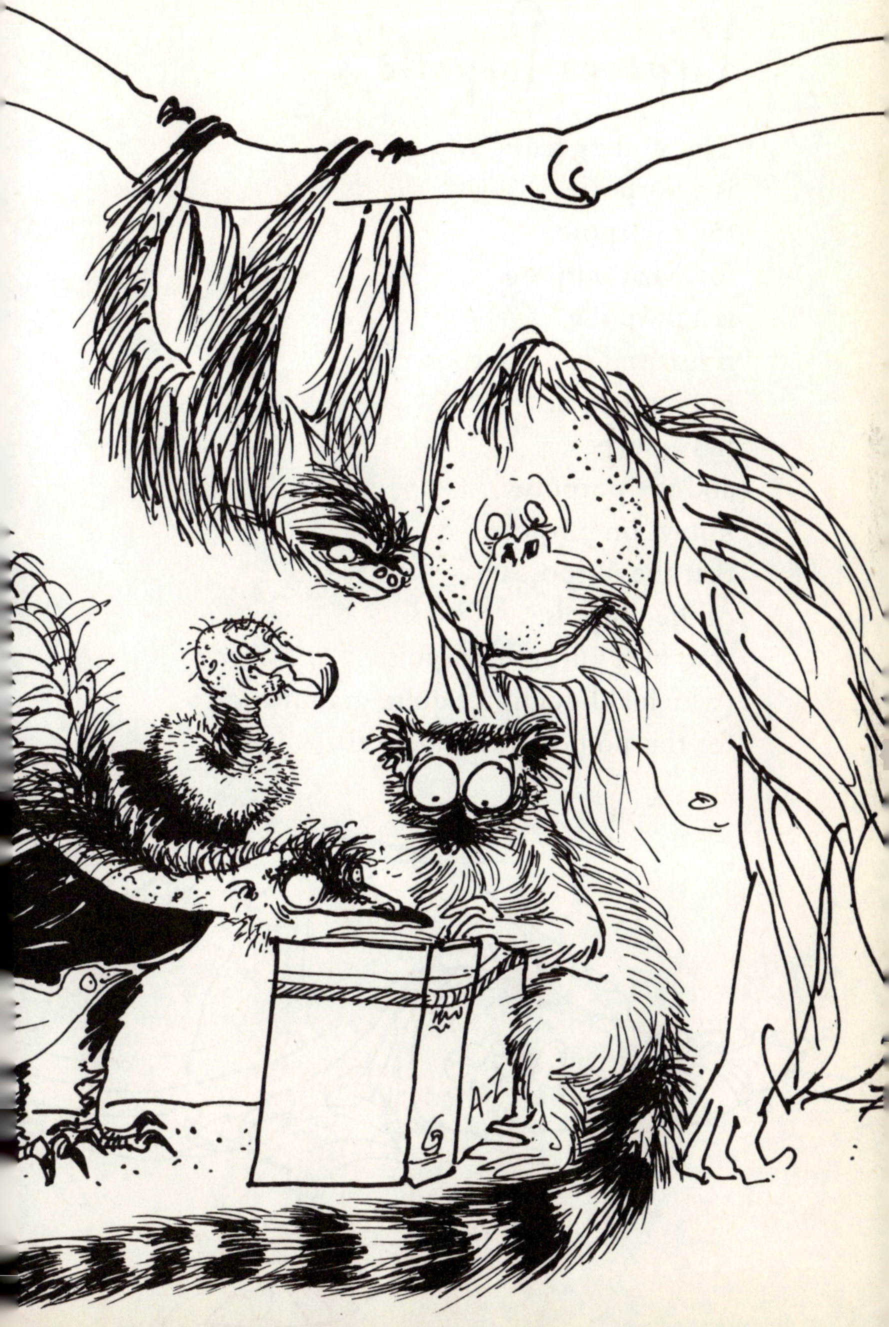
A-Z

Purpose Porpoise

The smiling harbour porpoise
is a porpoise
for a purpose
for what purpose
is a porpoise
if it hasn't got a purpose?
but a porpoise
has a purpose
and the porpoise
knows on purpose
that the purpose
of the porpoise
is to be a purpose porpoise
(which although not quite grammatical
for this poipose it is practical).

The Wolf

The lone wolf
may cry wolf
wolf all that and more
play one in sheep's clothing
keep one from the door.

Eggs a-Poppin'

These eggs belong to Myrtle
a very fertle turtle.

About the Author

Celeste Walters has been a primary and secondary schoolteacher, an art gallery director, a children's theatre actor/manager and a lecturer in drama and language and literature. Currently she divides her year between Melbourne and country New South Wales where she writes full-time.

Miss Walters, who has also written under her married name of Sowden, has published playscripts for children and adults, children's novels, and texts on developmental drama and the writing of eulogies. *Who's Who at the Zoo* is her third book of whimsical verse.

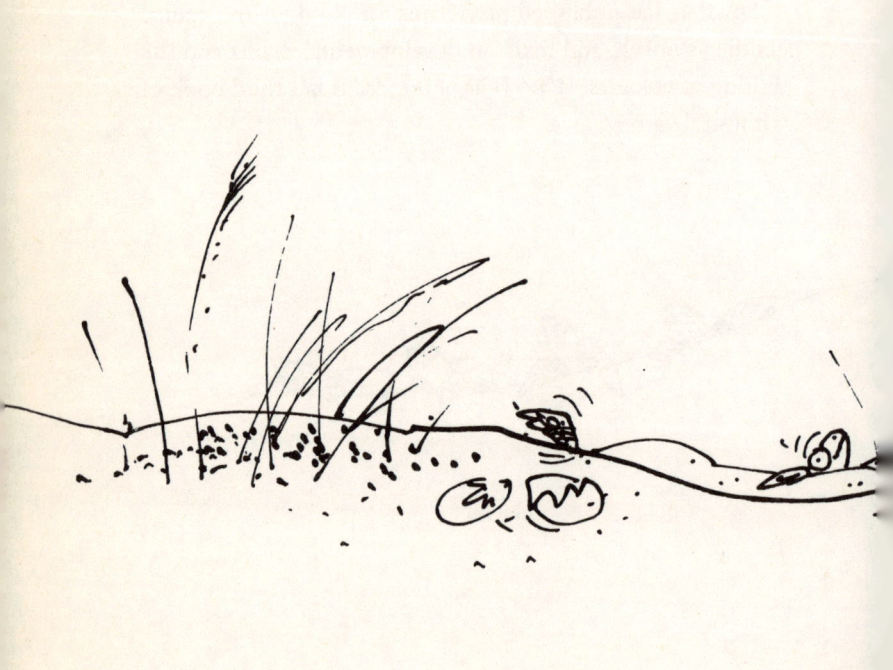

About the Illustrator

Patricia Mullins has lived with a menagerie of wonderful creatures since childhood. They have inspired many of her illustrations and have inevitably appeared in the numerous picture books she has illustrated since graduating from art school with a Fellowship of Illustration (RMIT) in the 1970s.

Animals have always been her favourite subjects and most recently have featured in her multi-award-winning book, *V for Vanishing, an Alphabet of Endangered Animals.* Like most of her picture books over the past ten years, the illustrations for *V for Vanishing* were done in tissue collage for which Mullins has been highly acclaimed both in Australia and the USA. However, her style remains versatile and she enjoys lino-cut, pastel, watercolour and line as well. *Who's Who at the Zoo* shows a return to the discipline of line and the fun of caricature with a keen observation of animals.

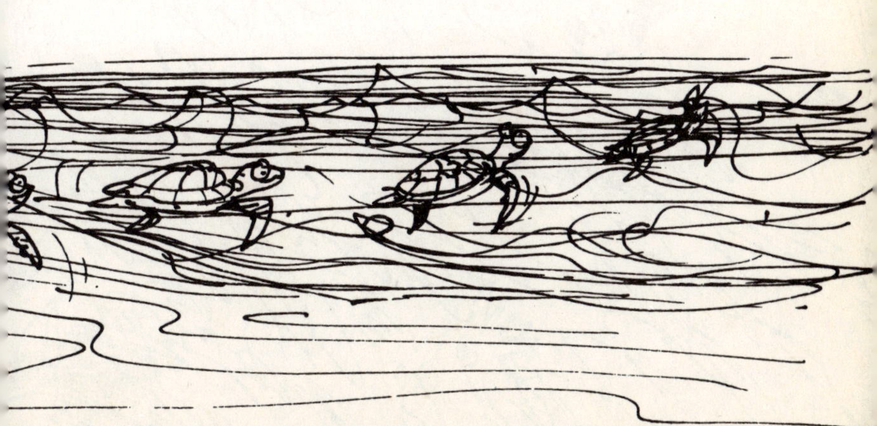

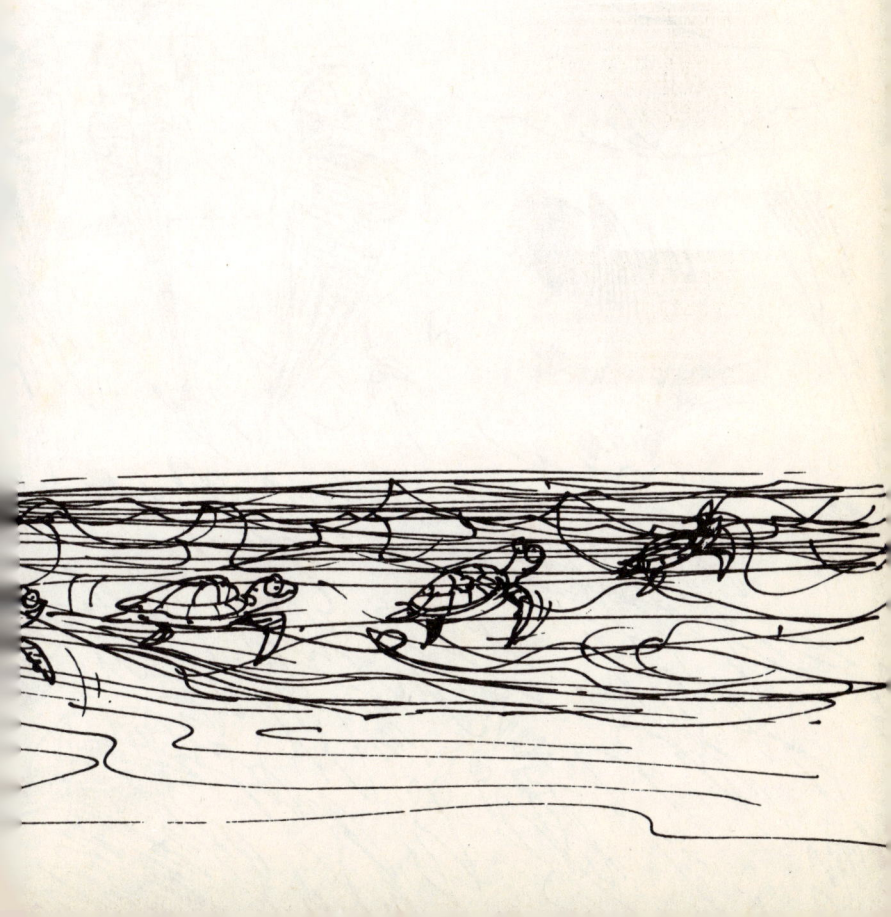

Doodle-oo!